# COCKTAIL
## Essentials

# COCKTAIL
## Essentials

### Alex Barker

Regency House Publishing Ltd.

# Contents

Published in 1996 by
**Regency House Publishing Limited**
The Grange
Grange Yard
London SE1 3AG

**Copyright © 1996 Regency House Publishing Limited**

ISBN 1 85361 448 3

Printed in China

**All photographs are supplied by Food Features.**

# Introduction

There are many opinions as to the origin of the word cocktail. Some say that it comes from the word *coquetier,* the French for egg-cup, which was about the same size as the glasses in which a miserly noblemen served drinks to his friends. Others say that during skirmishes between their two countries, an American general met King Axolotl VIII of Mexico and was offered a convivial drink by a beautiful young lady named Coctel. Another possible source is a Bordeaux wine cup given to French officers serving in America, called a *coquetel.* But the likeliest and most evocative is *cock-ale* – a mixture of spirits fed to fighting cocks in the 18th century to inflame them and encourage them on. The same mixture would also have been consumed by the punters, the number of tail feathers in their glasses indicating the number of different ingredients in the drinks.

The cocktail as we now know it had its roots in the twenties and thirties in America, possibly as a result of the Prohibition laws which led to the production of illicit home-made liquor or *moonshine* of dubious quality which, in order to make it palatable, required the addition of added flavourings. These drinks were gradually refined and many cocktails began to be created in honour of a special occasion, or a famous person, with many of them becoming classic drinks in their own right.

Although cocktails frequently contain more than one type of alcohol, the other ingredients – sugar, fruit, fruit juices, syrups, mixers and ice – play a crucial part. Much of the fun and adventure of mixing cocktails lies in the variety of taste and colour which can be created. If the idea appeals, it is worthwhile investing in a few basic ingredients before you start:

- Lemons, oranges, limes, tomato juice, glacé cherries, olives and mint are the most popular additions: others, such as pineapple, banana or mango are required for specific drinks.
- Colourful but non-alcoholic syrups such as grenadine – green or red.
- Mixers – soda water, tonic water, lemonade and ginger ale.
- Sweet and dry vermouths (red and white).
- Crème de cassis, crème de menthe and curaçao – the colourful liqueurs.
- A good mixture of spirits – brandy, fruit brandies, bourbon, rye, Cointreau, Drambuie, gin, tequila, vodka, whisky and rum (light and dark).
- Herbal and uniquely flavoured liqueurs such as Amaretto, Chartreuse, Galliano, kümmel.

- Coffee and nut liqueurs for occasional use – Kahlua, Malibu, Tia Maria.
- Wine, both sparkling and still, and cider.

Mixing a cocktail may sound simple but a few words of advice will help you to produce excellent mixed drinks every time.

- Invest in a shaker, larger rather than smaller, to allow the ingredients to be well incorporated. You could start off by using two very large sturdy tumblers, fitting one over the other. For a single cocktail, one large glass would suffice with a suitable lid or cover for shaking. It is important to remember, however, that the more vigorously you shake, the quicker the drink cools, and the slower the ice will melt, diluting the cocktail.
- Always have plenty of ice on hand. To crush ice, whizz the lumps very briefly in a food processor or blender. Alternatively, place it in a polythene bag and smash it with a rolling pin.
- Never use the same ice twice for different drinks.
- Chill the glasses if possible. For an interesting effect, dip the rims in beaten egg white and then caster sugar, or even salt (*see* Margarita on page 19).
- It is important that quantities are combined in correct proportions in order to achieve a good balance of taste, especially for shorts, so use the same measure throughout, using halves, quarters or other proportions of that measure as the recipe indicates. You can buy cocktail measures, but these are not strictly necessary. You could just as well use a small tumbler, glass, or even an egg cup. A standard pub measure is one-sixth of a gill, just less than one fluid ounce or about 2 tablespoonfuls.
- Collect a stock of different glasses and suitable decorations, straws, cocktail sticks etc.
- Cocktails are made in small quantities, enough to serve one unless otherwise stated.

## Alexander

There are several quite different versions of the Alexander cocktail, one based on gin, one on rye whiskey and Bénédictine and this one which is based on brandy.

**1 measure brandy**
**1 measure crème de cacao**
**1 measure cream**
**ice**
**grated nutmeg**

*Vigorously shake the three ingredients together with crushed ice, strain into a cocktail glass and sprinkle with nutmeg if you wish.*

## American Beauty

**¹/₃ measure brandy**
**¹/₃ measure dry vermouth**
**¹/₃ measure orange juice**
**2 dashes crème de menthe (white)**
**ice**
**port**

*Shake the first four ingredients together over ice and strain into a classic cocktail glass. Carefully pour one small tablespoonful or layer of port over the top.*

## Americano

**1 measure Campari**
**1 measure sweet vermouth**
**ice**
**soda water**
**twist of lemon**

*Pour the Campari and vermouth over ice in a tall tumbler or highball glass. Stir well, add soda to taste and a twist of lemon rind.*

*Left: Antonio*

*Brandy Alexander*

*Bartender*

## Balalaika

$^1/_3$ **measure Cointreau**
$^1/_3$ **measure vodka**
$^1/_3$ **measure lemon juice**
**ice**

*Shake all three over ice and strain into a cocktail glass.*

## Bartender

$^1/_4$ **measure dry vermouth**
$^1/_4$ **measure gin**
$^1/_4$ **measure Dubonnet**
$^1/_4$ **measure sherry**
**dash of Grand Marnier**
**ice**

*Shake everything together over ice and strain into a cocktail glass.*

*Black Russian*

## Antonio

$^1/_3$ **measure brandy**
$^1/_3$ **measure gin**
$^1/_6$ **measure maraschino**
$^1/_6$ **measure crème de menthe**
**ice**

*Shake the four ingredients together over ice and strain into a cocktail glass.*

## Applejack

$^1/_2$ **measure apple brandy**
$^1/_2$ **measure sweet vermouth**
**2 dashes angostura bitters**
**ice**
**olive or piece of lemon peel**

*Stir first three ingredients together over ice, strain into a cocktail glass and finish with an olive on a stick or a twist of peel.*

*Blue Star*

## Between-the-Sheets

$^2/_3$ **measure brandy**

$^2/_3$ **measure Cointreau**

$^2/_3$ **measure white rum**

**1 dash lemon juice**

**ice**

*Shake everything over ice and strain into a cocktail glass.*

## Black Russian

**1 measure black coffee**

**2 measures vodka**

**ice**

*Pour both together over ice and stir briskly.*

## Blue Star

$^1/_5$ **measure blue curaçao**

$^1/_3$ **measure gin**

$^1/_4$ **measure Lillet**

$^1/_6$ **measure orange juice**

**ice**

**lemon or lime slices**

*Shake together over ice, strain into a cocktail glass and decorate with the fruit slices.*

*Five-Fifteen (left) and Bolo Cocktail*

## Bolo Cocktail

This mixture of fresh fruit juice, well spiced and laced with a spirit, usually rum, was drunk in the 18th century.

**juice of $\frac{1}{4}$ lemon or $\frac{1}{2}$ lime**
**juice of $\frac{1}{2}$ orange**
**1 measure rum**
**1 teaspoon sugar**
**slices of orange**
**glacé cherries**

*Shake liquids with sugar over ice and strain into a cocktail glass. Finish off with slices of orange and cherries on a cocktail stick.*

---

## Bronx Cocktail

This drink was originally made with 'bathtub' gin, of very dubious quality! There are several versions of Bronx – there's the Golden, the Silver, the Terrace and the Empress. However, all are variations on this basic combination. Whisked-up egg white is an optional extra.

**$\frac{1}{2}$ measure gin**
**$\frac{1}{6}$ measure dry vermouth**
**$\frac{1}{6}$ measure sweet vermouth**
**$\frac{1}{6}$ orange juice**

*Shake all ingredients over ice and strain into a cocktail glass.*

*Bronx*

*Daiquiri*

## Cherry Blossom

There is an actual cherry blossom liqueur made from Japanese cherry blossoms which has a delicate pink colour and a wonderful perfume. This cocktail has a similar colour but rather more kick!

*Serves 4*
**4 measures brandy**
**5 measures cherry brandy**
**1 measure grenadine**
**1 measure lemon juice**
**1 measure curaçao**

*Shake everything over ice and strain into four glasses.*

## Daiquiri

Daiquiri acquired its name from an old nickel mine in Cuba, where drink was limited. So workers invented their own concoction using the local rum. There are many versions, usually based on white rum and lemon or lime juice. This recipe is more unusual and is served over crushed ice.

**$1\frac{1}{2}$ measures light rum**
**$\frac{1}{2}$ measure strawberry liqueur**
**$\frac{1}{4}$ measure grenadine**
**juice of $\frac{1}{2}$ lime**
**ice**
**strawberry or maraschino cherry**

*Mix liquids vigorously over ice. Strain into sugar-rimmed glasses and finish with a strawberry or a cherry on a stick.*

## Fallen Angel

1 dash angostura bitters
2 dashes crème de menthe
juice of 1 lemon or lime
2 measures gin
ice

*Shake well over ice and strain into a
cocktail glass.*

## Five-Fifteen

$^1/_3$ measure blue curaçao
$^1/_3$ measure dry vermouth
$^1/_3$ measure sweet cream
ice

*Shake well over ice and strain into a
cocktail glass.*

## Fox Trot

juice of $^1/_2$ lemon or 1 lime
2 dashes orange curaçao
2 measures light rum
ice

*Shake well over ice and strain into a
cocktail glass.*

## Gin Sling

This is a classic which has many variations.
Vary it to suit your palate.

juice of $^1/_3$ lemon
$^1/_2$ tbsp caster sugar
1 measure gin
ice
angostura bitters
slice of lemon

*Pour the lemon, sugar and gin over ice in a
highball glass and mix well. Top up with
fresh chilled water and float a dash of
angostura bitters carefully on the top.*

Gin Sling

## Gloom Chaser

1 measure dry vermouth
$1^1/_2$ measures gin
$^1/_2$ teaspoon grenadine
2 dashes Pernod
ice

*Shake well over ice and strain into a
cocktail glass.*

## Good Night Ladies

$^1/_6$ measure apricot brandy
$^1/_6$ measure grenadine
$^1/_2$ measure gin
$^1/_6$ measure lemon juice
ice

*Shake well over ice and strain into a glass.*

## Harvey Wallbanger

1 measure vodka
2 measures fresh orange juice
ice
$^1/_2$ measure Galliano
slice of orange
straw

*Shake the vodka and orange with ice. Strain
into a cocktail glass and pour on the
Galliano so that it floats on the top. Finish
with a slice of orange and serve with a straw.*

*Harvey Wallbanger*

## High Flyer

²/₃ measure gin

¹/₄ measure Strega

¹/₈ measure Van der Hum

lemon rind

ice

*Shake well over ice and strain into a cocktail glass. Finish off with a twist of lemon rind.*

## Jockey Club Special

¹/₄ measure gin

¹/₈ measure white crème de noyau

juice ¹/₂ lemon

2 dashes orange bitters

2 dashes angostura bitters

ice

*Shake all the ingredients over ice and strain into a cocktail glass.*

## Jupiter

1 teaspoon orange juice

1 teaspoon Parfait Amour liqueur

¹/₃ measure dry vermouth

²/₃ measure gin

ice

*Shake well over ice and strain into a cocktail glass.*

## The Kicker

2 dashes sweet vermouth

¹/₃ measure calvados or apple brandy

²/₃ measure light rum

ice

*Shake well over ice and strain into a glass.*

*Manhattan*

## Loch Lomond

1¹/₂ measures Scotch whisky

1 measure gomme syrup

3 dashes angostura bitters

ice

*Shake well over ice and serve on the rocks*

## Mai Tai

2 measures white rum

1 measure curaçao

1 measure fresh lime juice

2 measures grenadine

¹/₂ teaspoon sugar

ice

slice of pineapple

cocktail cherry

*Shake well over ice and strain into a glass with fresh ice. Finish off with the pineapple and cherry.*

## Manhattan Dry

This original dry version is reputed to have been invented in Maryland as a quick reviver for a wounded duellist in 1846. In the New York of the 1890s, sweet vermouth was added and the drink was named after the fashionable part of town.

**$^1/_2$ measure rye**
**$^1/_2$ measure dry vermouth**
**1 dash angostura bitters**
**ice**
**1 olive**

*Stir first three ingredients over ice, strain into a cocktail glass and finish with an olive.*

## Manhattan Sweet

**$^1/_2$ measure Canadian whisky**
**$^1/_2$ measure Italian (sweet) vermouth**
**2 dashes curaçao**
**1 dash angostura bitters**
**ice**
**cherry & a piece of orange peel**

*Stir the four liquids over ice, strain into a cocktail glass and finish with a cherry and a piece of peel.*

## Margarita

This classic cocktail is one of the few served with the glass rimmed with salt, guaranteed to give a unique burst of flavour.

**slices of lime**
**salt**
**$1^1/_2$ measures tequila**
**1 measure lime juice**
**$^1/_2$ measure Cointreau**
**ice**

*To prepare the glass, rub the rim with a cut lime and dip it into salt. Mix the remaining ingredients well over ice and strain into the glass. Serve with a slice of lime.*

*Margarita*

## Martini

This drink is virtually neat gin but with a slight but subtle hint of the other ingredient.

It is sometimes said that a real Martini cocktail should only be shown the vermouth bottle or just have the cork wafted over the glass. One story tells of a New York barman who was said to put neat gin into a cocktail glass, take a mouthful of vermouth, and then whisper the word 'vermouth' over the glass.

A simple way of adding only a hint of flavour is to merely swirl a few drops round the glass and then pour it away!

**3 measures dry gin**
**1 measure dry vermouth or less**
**green olives on sticks**

*Stir gin and vermouth together with plenty of ice, strain and pour into a chilled glass. Serve with a green olive.*

*Martini*

## Moonlight

*Serves 4*

**3 measures grapefruit juice**
**4 measures gin**
**1 measure kirsch**
**4 measures white wine**
**ice**
**thin peelings of lemon rind**

*Shake over ice, strain into glasses and finish with a twist of lemon peel.*

## My Fair Lady

**1 measure gin**
**$^1/_2$ measure lemon juice**
**$^1/_2$ measure orange juice**
**1 teaspoon fraise liqueur**
**1 egg white**
**ice**

*Shake all the ingredients well over ice and strain into a cocktail glass.*

*Moonlight*

*Negroni*

*My Fair Lady*

*Nightcap Flip*

## Old Fashioned

*Created for racegoers at Louisville's Pendennis club, this cocktail was popularized during the prohibition era disguised with fruit.*

**1 lump of sugar**
**2 dashes angostura bitters**
**ice**
**2 measures bourbon**

*Place the sugar and bitters in a heavy tumbler and crush the sugar. Add an ice cube and a slice of orange. Stir in the bourbon and serve with a spoon.*

## Palm Beach

**²/₃ measure gin**
**¹/₆ measure dry vermouth**
**¹/₆ measure grapefruit juice**
**ice**

*Shake well over ice and strain into a cocktail glass.*

## Parisian Blonde

**¹/₃ measure curaçao**
**¹/₃ measure Jamaican rum**
**¹/₃ measure cream**
**ice**

*Shake well over ice and strain into a cocktail glass.*

## Pink Gin

This drink was invented by Royal Navy surgeons for medicinal purposes. It helped to keep Sir Francis Chichester optimistic on his long solo voyage around the world.

**1¹/₂ measures gin**
**2 dashes angostura bitters**

*Stir gently and do not ice.*

Pink Gin

## Negroni

**¹/₃ measure gin**
**¹/₃ measure sweet vermouth**
**¹/₃ measure Campari**
**ice**
**twist of lemon**

*Shake three liquids over ice, strain into a cocktail glass and finish with a twist of lemon rind.*

## Nightcap Flip

There are several nightcap cocktails which are hot and soothing. This one has a little more of a kick!

**¹/₃ measure brandy**
**¹/₃ measure anisette**
**¹/₃ measure blue curaçao**
**yolk of one egg**
**ice**
**maraschino cherry**

*Vigorously shake first four ingredients over ice and strain into a cocktail glass. Finish with a cherry on a stick.*

*Salome*

## Rusty Nail

1$^1/_2$ measures Scotch whisky

$^1/_2$ measure Drambuie

ice

twist of lemon

*Stir over ice and finish off with a twist of lemon rind.*

---

## Salome

$^1/_3$ measure gin

$^1/_3$ measure white Dubonnet

$^1/_3$ measure dry vermouth

maraschino cherry

*Stir over ice and strain into a cocktail glass. Finish with a maraschino cherry.*

---

## Sand-Martin

$^2/_3$ measure gin

$^2/_3$ measure Italian vermouth

$^1/_5$ measure green Chartreuse

ice

*Shake well over ice and strain into a cocktail glass.*

---

## Screwdriver

1 measure vodka

2 measures fresh orange juice

ice

*Shake well over ice and strain into a cocktail glass.*

---

## Shamrock

$^1/_2$ measure Irish whiskey

$^1/_2$ measure dry vermouth

3 dashes crème de menthe

3 dashes green Chartreuse

*Stir over ice and strain into a cocktail glass.*

Snowball

## Sidecar

$^1/_3$ measure brandy

$^1/_3$ measure Cointreau

$^1/_3$ measure lemon juice

ice

*Shake over ice and strain into a cocktail glass.*

## Snowball

$^1/_6$ measure crème de violette

$^1/_6$ measure anisette

$^1/_6$ measure crème de menthe

$^1/_6$ measure sweetened cream

$^1/_3$ measure gin

ice

*Shake all the ingredients well together over ice and strain into a cocktail glass.*

## Sputnik

1 measure vodka
1 measure cream
1 teaspoon maraschino
ice
maraschino cherry

*Shake ingredients over ice and strain into a cocktail glass. Finish off with a cherry.*

## Tequila Sunrise

Tequila is a spirit made from a type of Mexican cactus known as mescal. There are two styles, silver and golden, both used as the bases of many cocktails, with this one named after its striking colour.

2 measures silver tequila
6 measures orange juice
2 measures grenadine

*Pour all the ingredients into a cocktail glass and stir gently. Add a few lumps of ice if you wish and sugar the rim of the glass for effect.*

## Vodkatini

2 measures vodka
1 measure dry vermouth
ice
twist of lemon peel

*Shake over ice, strain into a cocktail glass and finish off with a twist of lemon.*

## Washington Cocktail

$^2/_3$ measure dry vermouth
$^1/_3$ measure brandy
2 dashes angostura bitters
2 dashes gomme syrup

*Shake well and strain into a cocktail glass.*

*Whiskey Sour*

## Whisky Mac

$^1/_3$ measure ginger wine
$^2/_3$ measure Scotch whisky

*Stir well and serve in a
cocktail glass.*

---

## Whiskey Sour

$^3/_4$ measure lemon or lime juice
$1^1/_2$ measures bourbon or rye
1 teaspoon caster sugar
ice
cherry and slice of orange

*Shake the ingredients well over ice, strain
into a small glass and decorate with a cherry
and a slice of orange.*

---

## White Lady

This can be made with vodka, but gin seems
to be more popular.

1 measure gin
$^1/_2$ measure lemon juice
$^1/_2$ measure Cointreau
dash egg white
slice of lemon or a cherry

*Shake very well over ice until frothy.
Then strain into a cocktail glass and finish
off with a slice of lemon or a cherry.*

*White Lady*

*Bloody Mary*

*The Collins (left) and Apple Fizz*

## Apple Fizz

**150ml (¼ pint) apple juice or cider**

**1 measure calvados**

**juice ½ lemon**

**½ egg white**

**pinch sugar**

**ice**

**slices of lemon**

*Shake well over ice until frothy and pour immediately into a highball glass. Finish with a slice of lemon and a cherry.*

## Bloody Mary

Variations on this popular cocktail are many. There's the Bullshot in which you replace the tomato juice with 4 measures of good beef bouillon or canned consommé: and the Clamato in which half a measure of clam juice replaces the lemon and seasonings. The South American version is called Bloody Maria in which tequila replaces the vodka.

**1½ measures vodka**

**2-3 measures tomato juice**

**good squeeze lemon juice**

**2 dashes Worcestershire sauce**

**celery salt**

**ice**

**stick of celery or small tomatoes**

*Shake thoroughly over ice and strain into a long glass. Finish off with a celery stick to stir or cherry tomatoes on a cocktail stick.*

## The Collins

This cocktail was named after a London head-waiter in the 19th century, John Collins. The difference between this and the Tom Collins cocktail is the type of gin used.

**juice ½ lemon**

**2 teaspoons caster sugar**

**2 measures Holland gin or Old Tom gin**

**ice**

**soda water**

**zest of lemon**

*Mix over ice in a small tumbler or highball glass and top up with soda. Finish with a piece of zest of lemon.*

## Cuba Libre

This well established cocktail is probably the drink referred to in the old song 'Rum and Coca-Cola'.

**1½ measures white rum**

**1 small bottle cola**

**ice**

**squeeze lime juice**

*Stir over ice in a small tumbler or highball glass and top with a squeeze of lime at the last minute.*

## Dubonnet Fizz

**1 measure Dubonnet**

**½ measure cherry brandy**

**2 tbsp lemon juice**

**2 tbsp orange juice**

**1 egg white**

**ice**

**soda water**

*Shake well over ice and strain into a glass. Top up with soda.*

*Right: Dubonnet Fizz*

*Gin Fizz*

## Gin Fizz

**1 ½ measures gin**

**1 teaspoon sugar**

**ice**

**soda water**

*Stir gin and sugar together with ice until the sugar dissolves, then top up with soda.*

---

## Royal Grand Fizz

**2 measures gin**

**juice ½ lemon**

**juice ½ orange**

**3 dashes sugar syrup**

**2 dashes maraschino**

**½ measure cream**

**ice**

**soda water**

*Shake all ingredients over ice and top up with soda water.*

*Royal Grand Fizz*

*Keep Sober*

## Leave it to Me

$^3/_5$ measure gin
$^1/_5$ measure dry vermouth
$^1/_5$ measure apricot brandy
2 dashes lemon juice
2 dashes grenadine
ice
soda

*Shake first five over ice, pour into a tall glass and top up with soda.*

## The Londoner

$1^1/_2$ measures gin
$^1/_2$ measure rosehip syrup
$^1/_2$ measure dry vermouth
juice $^1/_2$ lemon
ice
soda water

*Pour over ice in a highball glass, stir and top up with soda.*

## Highland Cooler

$^1/_2$ teaspoon sugar
ice
$1^1/_3$ measures whisky
ginger ale
twist or spiral of lemon rind

*Mix sugar and a little water in a small highball glass. Add ice, the whisky, and top up with ginger ale. Finish off with orange peel.*

## Keep Sober

1 measure grenadine
1 measure fresh lemon or lime juice
ice
lemonade or tonic water
maraschino cherries
lemon rind or peel

*Pour the grenadine and lemon juice over ice into a small highball glass or tumbler. Top up with lemonade, maraschino cherries and a piece of lemon peel.*

## Million Dollars

1 teaspoon grenadine
1 egg white
$^1/_3$ measure sweet vermouth
$^2/_3$ measure gin
2-3 measures pineapple juice
ice

*Shake well over ice and strain into a medium-size glass.*

*Mint Julep*

*Million Dollars*

## Mint Julep

Juleps originated, like many other drinks, in very hot climates where long, cool drinks were necessary and mint was found to be both soothing and relaxing. It can be successfully made with other spirits too.

**5-6 sprigs fresh mint**
**1-2 teaspoons caster sugar**
**2 measures bourbon or rye**
**ice**
**soda water**
**sprig of mint**

*Crush the mint leaves and sugar together in a long tumbler or highball glass. Add the spirit, fill the glass with ice and top up with soda water. Finish off with a sprig of mint.*

## Moscow Mule

**2 measures vodka**
**1 measure lime juice**
**ice**
**ginger beer**
**sprig of mint**

*Stir vodka and lime juice over ice in a highball glass. Fill up with ginger beer and finish with a sprig of mint.*

## Perry Highball

**1 lump of ice**
**2 measures whisky**
**cider or perry**

*Pour the whisky over the ice in a highball glass and top up with the cider.*

*Pimm's No 1*

*Widow's Kiss*

## Pimm's No.1

1 measure Pimm's No.1
4 measures lemonade
(for a less sweet version mix in a little dry
ginger or cola)
ice
slices of apple, orange and cucumber
sprigs of mint or borage
straw

*Pour the liquids over ice in a highball glass.
Add the fruit and sprig of mint or borage,
and serve with a straw.*

## Pimm's Royal

*The same as above but mixed with
champagne instead of lemonade*

## Pina Colada

1¹⁄₂ measures rum
2 measures pineapple juice
ice
1 measure coconut cream
piece of pineapple and a glacé cherry to
decorate

*Shake well over ice, then strain into a glass
or an empty coconut shell. Finish off with
the pineapple and a cherry on a stick and
drink through a straw.*

## Rickey

*Thought to have been created in the
Shoomaker's Bar of Washington D.C. for a
well-known lobbyist nicknamed Colonel Jim
Rickey though his real name was Joe.*

2 measures gin
1 teaspoon grenadine
¹⁄₂ fresh lime
ice
soda

*Pour gin and grenadine over ice in a tumbler*

*or highball. Add the lime juice and lime peel,
then top up with soda.*

## Santa Cruz Daisy

3 dashes sugar syrup
2 or 3 dashes maraschino or curaçao
juice of ¹⁄₂ small lemon
2 measures rum
shaved or crushed ice
soda or carbonated water

*Shake the liquids over ice, strain into a
tumbler and top up with the water.*

## Singapore Sling

1 ¹⁄₂ measures gin
juice 1 lemon
1 teaspoon caster sugar
ice
soda water
¹⁄₂ measure Cointreau
¹⁄₂ measure cherry brandy
slice of lemon

*Mix gin, lemon and sugar over ice in a tall
highball glass. Add Cointreau, cherry brandy
and soda water. Stir well. Decorate with a
slice of lemon and drink with a straw.*

## Widow's Kiss

¹⁄₄ measure Bénédictine
¹⁄₄ measure Chartreuse
¹⁄₂ measure calvados
dash angostura bitters
ice, soda water

*Stir liquids with ice in a tall glass. Add a
small amount of soda water.*

## Black Velvet

*There is also a poor man's version of this drink, made with cider instead of champagne, and is a great long drink.*

**stout or Guinness, chilled
champagne, chilled**

*Pour equal amounts of stout and champagne carefully together into a tall tumbler or highball glass.*

## Bombay Punch

*The secret of a good punch is that, in the end, no one flavour should dominate. It makes an excellent party drink.*

**Serves 18-20 large glasses
600ml/1 pint brandy
600ml/1 pint sherry
1 measure maraschino
1 measure orange curaçao
2.4 litres/4 pints champagne
(or sparkling white wine)
1.2 litres/2 pints carbonated water
cracked ice
fruits to slice for decoration**

*Stir all the ingredients, except the ice, together in a punchbowl or large container. Surround the bowl with cracked ice until chilled and then decorate with fruit.*

## Buck's Fizz

**1 measure fresh orange juice,
chilled champagne or sparkling white
wine, chilled**

*Pour the orange juice into a tall flute and fill up with champagne to taste.*

*Black Velvet*

*Strawberry Champagne Cocktail*

## Champagne Cocktail

**1 cube sugar**
**angostura bitters**
**1 teaspoon brandy (optional)**
**champagne, chilled**
**strawberry (optional)**

*Put the sugar cube in a champagne flute and pour on a few drops of bitters. Add the brandy too if you wish. Pour on the champagne and serve with a strawberry.*

## Cranbury Perry

**3 measures cranberry juice, chilled**
**2-3 measures white sparkling wine,**
**sparkling perry, or muscatel, chilled**
**fruit to decorate**

*Pour the juice and wine or perry together into a chilled wine glass and decorate.*

## Death in the Afternoon

The rumour goes that this was Ernest Hemingway's favourite drink when he lived in Paris.

**1 measure Pernod**
**chilled brut champagne**
**ice cubes**

*Put two ice cubes in a champagne flute and pour the Pernod over them. Carefully pour in the champagne, stir gently and drink before the bubbles disappear.*

*Cranberry Perry*

*Kir*

# Kir

The character of this drink depends on your taste for blackcurrant; a few drops may suffice, but you can add more to taste.

**few drops cassis (blackcurrant liqueur)**
**white Burgundy, chilled**

*Pour a very little cassis into the base of a wine glass and swill it around. Pour in the wine, it should need no mixing. Serve.*

# Kir Royale

*The same as above but with champagne substituted for the white wine.*

# Manhattan Cooler

**juice of $^1/_2$ lemon or lime**
**$^1/_2$ teaspoon caster sugar**
**2 measures claret**
**3 dashes rum**
**fruit in season to decorate**

*Stir well together over ice and strain into medium-sized glasses. Decorate.*

# Pineapple Julep
**Serves 6**
**plenty of crushed ice**
**juice of 2 oranges**
**2 measures raspberry vinegar**
**2 measures maraschino**
**3 measures gin**
**bottle sparkling Moselle or**
**Saumur white wine**
**1 small ripe pineapple cut into pieces**

*Stir everything thoroughly in a tall jug and serve before the ice melts totally.*

## Prince of Wales

**ice cubes**
**1 measure brandy**
**1 measure Madeira wine or muscatel**
**three drops curaçao**
**2 dashes angostura bitters**
**champagne brut, chilled**

*Shake all together, except for the champagne,*
*and strain into a chilled champagne flute.*
*Top up with champagne. Finish with a slice*
*of orange.*

## Sangria

This makes an excellent long, cold summer
party drink if you add the lemonade, but can
just as easily be made in small quantities.

*Serves 6-8*
**juice of 1 orange**
**juice of 1 lemon**
**2 tbsp caster sugar**
**ice**
**1 orange, thinly sliced**
**1 lemon thinly sliced**
**1 bottle red wine, chilled**
**lemonade to taste (optional)**

*Stir the orange and lemon juice with sugar in*
*a large bowl or jug until it dissolves. Add the*
*ice and the sliced fruit and then pour in the*
*wine. Top up with lemonade to taste.*

*A Jug of Sangria with a Pineapple Julep and a Collins in the foreground*

# Flips and Nogs

## Ale Flip

This hot ale brew is very similar to the Scottish Het Pint which also has whisky added.

**1.2 litres/2 pints ale**
**2 egg whites**
**4 egg yolks**
**4 tbsp soft brown sugar**
**plenty of grated nutmeg**

*Put the ale in a pan and bring it slowly to the boil. Beat the yolks and the whites separately. Gradually add them into the sugar and flavour with nutmeg. When well mixed, gently and gradually pour on the boiling ale, beating constantly. Now the mixture should be poured rapidly from one jug to another until you have a fine, smooth froth. Drink immediately.*

## Angel's Advocaat

Advocaat is a ready-made liqueur of egg yolks, sugar, vanilla and brandy. However, it can be used to create wonderfully colourful combinations with gentle mixing and a steady hand. Here are three variations on the egg nog to suit different tastes.

*Serves 3*
**1 egg white**
**4 measures advocaat**
**1 measure Cointreau**
**ice**
**1 measure of either crème de menthe,**
**Dubonnet or port**
**maraschino cherries**

*Shake the egg white, advocaat and Cointreau together until frothy. Place an ice cube and the Dubonnet or port in a chilled cocktail glass and carefully pour on one third of the*

*advocaat mixture. You could also sugar the rims of the glasses with different coloured sugars before filling with the cocktail. Decorate with cherries, slices of orange or umbrellas.*

## Baltimore Egg Nog

**1 egg**
**1 teaspoon sugar**
**1 measure Madeira**
**¼ measure brandy**
**¼ measure dark rum**
**milk**
**ice**
**grated nutmeg**

*Shake the egg, wine, spirits and a little milk over ice. Strain into a large tumbler and top with grated nutmeg.*

## Egg Nog

This is the simplest version which is well known to settle an upset stomach and is a perfect pick-me-up when convalescing.

**1 egg**
**1 tbsp caster sugar**
**2 measures any preferred spirit**
**ice**
**milk**

*Shake first three ingredients together over ice, strain into a long tumbler and top up with the chilled milk.*

## Pink Pussyfoot

**1 measure lemon juice**
**1 measure orange juice**
**2-3 strawberries, mashed**

**1 measure fraise**
**½ egg yolk**
**dash of pink grenadine**
**ice**
**sprig of mint and strawberry to finish**

*Shake all the ingredients together over ice very vigorously. Pour into a cocktail glass and finish off with the mint or a strawberry.*

## Porto Flip

**1 egg**
**½ tbsp caster sugar**
**2 measures port**
**little milk**
**grated fresh nutmeg**

*Shake well together and serve in a medium-sized glass finished with grated nutmeg. Do not chill. If preferred, the port can be slightly warmed.*

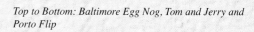

*Top to Bottom: Baltimore Egg Nog, Tom and Jerry and Porto Flip*

## Rum Noggin

A noggin is an old English liquid measure which is equal to a gill or 5 fluid ounces. It is also a term for a small mug, which is probably the best thing from which to drink a noggin or two.

*Serves 12*
**12 eggs**
**8-12 teaspoons caster sugar**
**1.2 litres/2 pints dark rum**
**2.4 litres/4 pints milk, cold or warm**
**grated fresh nutmeg**

*Beat the eggs in a punch bowl and add the sugar, stirring until dissolved. Stir in the rum and then the milk. Sprinkle with nutmeg and serve.*

## Thunder and Lightning

**$^1/_5$ measure cognac**
**1 egg yolk**
**2 dashes grenadine**
**ice**
**cayenne pepper**

*Shake well together and strain into a medium-sized glass. Top with a shake of cayenne pepper.*

## Tom and Jerry

**$^1/_6$ measure Jamaican rum**
**$^1/_6$ measure brandy**
**1 egg, beaten**
**hot water or milk**
**sugar**

*Gently stir all together and serve hot or cold.*

*Pink Pussyfoot*

*Right: Cranberry and Orange Chill*

46

# Fruity Numbers

*Apple Cup*

*Avocado Cooler*

## Cinderella Cocktail

$^1/_3$ measure orange juice

$^1/_3$ measure lemon juice

$^1/_3$ measure pineapple juice

ice

glacé cherry

mint

*Shake everything with ice and finish off with a cherry and sprig of mint.*

## Cranberry and Orange Chill

juice of 2 blood oranges

150ml/$^1/_4$ pint cranberry juice

2tbsp blackcurrant syrup

ice

slice of orange or piece of pineapple

*Mix well over ice and finish with a slice of orange or wedge of pineapple.*

## Fruit Punch

2 measures orange juice

2 measures grapefruit juice

2 measures pineapple juice

2 measures apple juice

few drops angostura bitters

ice

slices of various fruits to decorate

*Mix all the liquids together and pour onto a highball half filled with ice. Add the fruit and drink with a straw.*

## Apple Cup

juice $^1/_2$ small lemon

1 measure calvados or brandy

few drops vanilla essence

150m/l$^1/_4$ pint apple juice, chilled

ice

slice of lemon or apple

*Mix all the ingredients together in a highball glass with ice and serve with a slice of lemon or apple.*

## Avocado Cooler

$^1/_2$ avocado

juice of $^1/_2$ lime

1 teaspoon sugar

$^1/_2$ measure dry vermouth

1 measure gin

ice, tonic water

*Blend the avocado, lime juice and sugar together. Shake with vermouth and gin over ice. Strain into a cocktail glass and top up with tonic water to taste.*

## Kiwi Cooler

1 kiwi, peeled and crushed

crushed ice

1 measure pineapple or passion fruit juice

150ml/$^1/_4$ pint lemonade

pieces of pineapple

*Shake everything together until well iced and frothy. Pour into a highball glass, finish off with a wedge of pineapple and drink through a straw.*

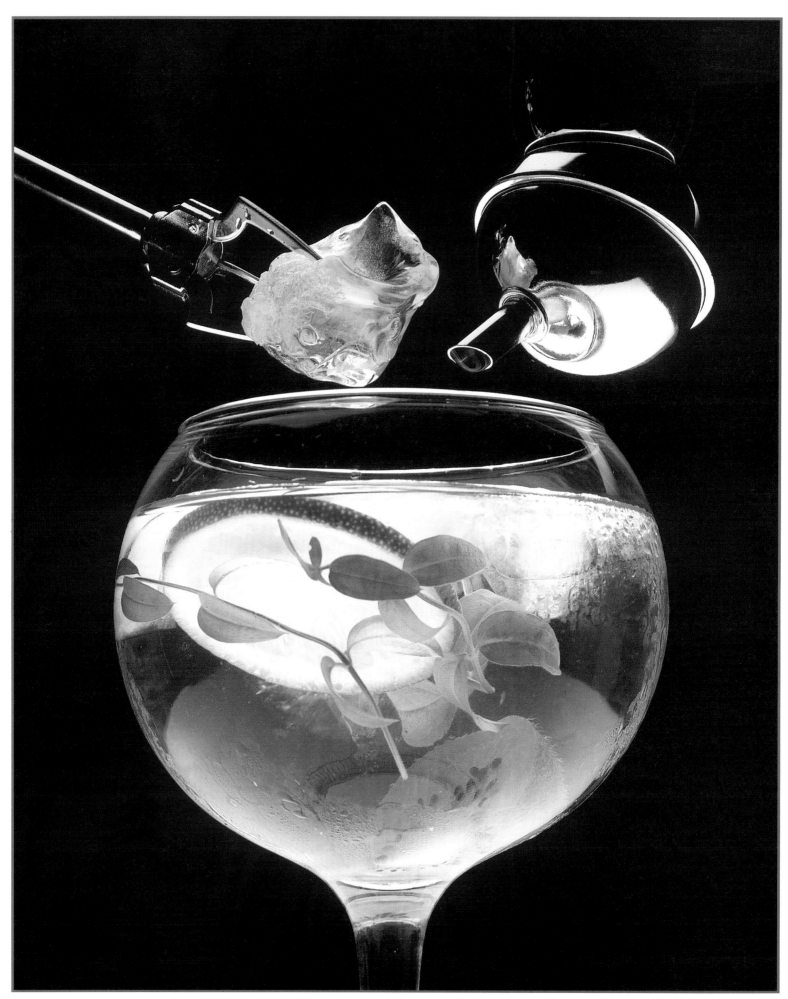

*Mint and Lime Refresher*

## Mint and Lime Refresher

**juice of 1 lime**
**few slices of cucumber and kiwi fruit**
**ice**
**sprigs of mint**
**carbonated water, iced**

*Mix the lime, cucumber and kiwi fruit in a highball glass with the ice and mint. Allow to marinade for 5-10 minutes before topping up with iced water.*

## Planter's Punch

*This must be every barman's favourite concoction as he adds his own variations and special touches to this classic.*

**1 measure dark rum**
**2 measures fresh orange juice**
**juice ¹/₂ lime**
**1 tbsp gomme syrup**
**dash of grenadine**
**crushed ice**
**cocktail cherry**
**slices of fruit**

*Shake together the liquid ingredients with the crushed ice. Strain into a medium-sized tumbler and finish with slices of fruit and a cherry or sprig of mint.*

*Planter's Punch*

## Raspberry Lemonade

Serves 4

2 lemons

110g/4oz caster sugar

110g/4oz fresh raspberries

few drops vanilla essence

crushed ice

carbonated water, iced

sprigs of lemon balm

*Trim the ends off the lemons, quarter them and place in a blender or processor with the sugar, raspberries, vanilla and ice. Blend for 2-3 minutes or until smooth. Sieve into tall glasses and top up with water. Decorate each glass with a sprig of lemon balm.*

## Redcurrant Shrub

1 pint/600ml redcurrant juice (made from approximately 1.3kg/3lb currants, well crushed and strained)

450g/1lb sugar

brandy or rum

*Stir the juice and sugar in a pan until the sugar has dissolved. Then bring to the boil and simmer gently for 8-10 minutes, spooning off any scum that forms. Allow to cool and then add 75ml (3 fluid ounces ) of brandy per pint of syrup in the pan. Bottle and leave to mature for 5-6 weeks.*

## Strawberry Crush

1 egg white

caster sugar

juice $^1/_2$ lemon

110g/4oz ripe strawberries

$^1/_4$ pint/150ml lemonade, chilled

crushed ice

sprig of mint

*Lightly whisk the egg and dip the rim of the glass into it. Then dip the rim into the lemon juice and set aside to set. Meanwhile, put aside a large strawberry for decoration and hull the rest. Place them in a blender or food processor along with the rest of the ingredients. Blend or process for 2-3 minutes until smooth but well frothed up. Pour into a glass and decorate with a whole or sliced strawberry.*

*Redcurrant Shrub*

*Winter Warmers*

## Athol Brose

A delicious Scottish combination which also forms the base of a rich pudding when whipped into thick cream.

**75g/3oz oatmeal**
**450ml/³/₄ pint water**
**2 tbsp runny heather honey**
**whisky**
**1-2 measures cream**

*Soak the oatmeal in the water until it forms a thick paste. Leave to stand for 30 minutes, then pass through a fine sieve, pressing with a wooden spoon to squeeze out as much of the liquid as possible into a bowl. Discard the oatmeal. Mix in the honey and pour into a quart bottle, filling up with whisky. Cork and store the brew for a day or two. Shake gently before pouring out, blend with a little cream and serve warmed through.*

## Apple Toddy

**1 measure whisky**
**3 measures cider or apple juice**
**1 slice lemon**

*Warm the whisky and apple juice gently together and pour into a medium-sized tumbler with a slice of lemon.*

## Bishop (or Archbishop)

*Serves 4*
**1 pint port**
**25g/1oz soft brown sugar**
**few cloves**
**2 oranges, sliced**

*In a small pan, heat the port with the sugar, cloves and orange slices. Serve in ready-heated glasses or mugs.*

## Glühwein

This hot mulled wine cup from the ski slopes of Europe has become a popular form of winter tipple.

*Serves 8-10*
**3 bottles red wine**
**a few pieces of lemon zest**
**good pinch each of ground ginger, cinnamon and cloves**
**(or use whole spices if you prefer but remember to remove them before serving)**
**50g/2oz sugar**

*Heat the wine in a stainless steel or non-stick saucepan with the zest, spices and sugar. When the sugar has dissolved and the wine is hot but not boiling, leave to infuse for 5-10 minutes before serving. Dilute with a little water to taste.*

*Opposite, left to right: Mulled Wine, Cider Cup and Hot Toddy*

*Above: Glühwein*

## Hot Toddy

**1 teaspoon sugar**
**a little boiling water**
**1 measure rum or brandy**
**1 twist lemon or orange peel**

*Dissolve the sugar in boiling water, then stir in the rum or brandy and heat through. Serve hot with a twist of lemon or orange peel.*

---

## Irish Coffee

This is thought to have been created by Joe Sheridan in the 1940s when he was head chef at Shannon Airport, Ireland.

**2 measures Irish whiskey**
**1 teaspoon sugar or to taste**
**freshly made strong black coffee**
**2 measures thick (double) cream**

*Put the whiskey into a warmed, large wine glass with the sugar. Pour in the coffee and stir. When the sugar has completely dissolved, dribble in the cream over the back of a spoon which is just touching the top of the coffee. Keep pouring until all the cream is added and has settled on the top. Do not stir, but drink the coffee through the cream.*

---

## Jaggaer Tae

**hot fresh tea without milk**
**sugar to taste**
**2 measures schnapps or brandy**
**slice of lemon**

*Pour the hot tea into a heated glass or mug and stir in sugar to taste until dissolved. Add the schnapps and finish with a slice of lemon. Serve very hot.*

*Jaggaer Tae*

*Irish Coffee*

# High in Health

There are times in the day, such as breakfast-time, when a refreshing and vitamin-rich cocktail is the first choice. Virtually all fruits and vegetables can be used for they all contain useful vitamins and minerals which are essential to our health and vitality. Be sure to use them immediately when they are at their peak of freshness and don't store them for long as the goodness is quickly lost. You do need a food processor or blender of some sort to get a good smooth result.

## Banana Breakfast Shake

**1 small banana**
**50g/2oz thick Greek-style natural yoghurt**
**1 free-range egg**
**1tbsp light brown sugar**
**ice**
**sprig of mint**

*Process the banana, yoghurt, egg and sugar in a blender with one or two lumps of ice for about 2 minutes. Pour into a tall glass garnished with a sprig of mint.*

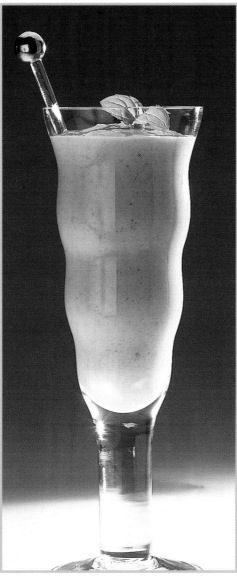
*Banana Breakfast Shake*

## Carrot Cocktail

**75g/3oz raw carrots, peeled and roughly chopped**
**1 slice pineapple, roughly chopped**
**1teaspoon lemon juice**
**1tbsp clear honey**
**ice**
**sprig of parsley or mint**

*Place the carrot, pineapple, lemon and honey in a blender and whizz for 1-2 minutes until smooth. Serve over ice with a sprig of parsley or mint.*

*Carrot Cocktail*

## Seven Veg Kick

*Serves 4*
**600ml/1pint tomato juice**
**1 stalk celery, diced**
**$^{1}/_{4}$ green pepper, chopped**
**$^{1}/_{4}$ yellow pepper, chopped**
**1 small sweet onion, chopped**
**2 small carrots, peeled and roughly chopped**
**3-4 florets cauliflower**
**juice and rind of $^{1}/_{2}$ lemon**
**salt and black pepper to taste**
**ice**
**parsley or coriander sprigs**

*Place all the ingredients, apart from the ice and herbs, into a blender and whizz until smooth. Sieve, if necessary, into long tumblers or highballs filled up with ice. Finish with a herb sprig.*

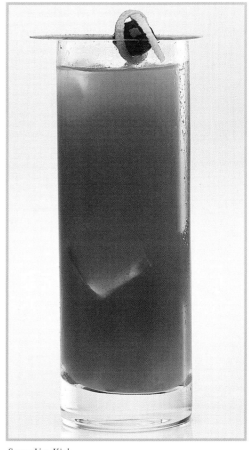
*Seven Veg Kick*

## Virgin Mary

You can't beat a glass of tomato juice, well flavoured with spices and a dash or two of a hot and spicy sauce. It serves well as a tonic and reviver at any time of the day.

**4 measures tomato juice**
**$^{1}/_{2}$ measure lemon juice**
**few dashes Worcestershire sauce, Tabasco sauce and celery salt**
**ice**
**leafy celery stick to stir**

*Mix the tomato, lemon and seasonings to taste until it has a really good kick. Pour into an ice-filled tumbler or highball and serve with a stick of celery for a final stir.*

*Virgin Mary*

There will be few who have not had that *'morning after the night before'* feeling! It usually goes, however, with a little fresh air and a long glass of orange juice. But when you have seriously overstepped the mark, and can't get your head off the pillow, you may feel the need for one of these.

## Cucumber Whizz

**$^{1}/_{4}$ cucumber, peeled**
**juice 1 lime**
**1 measure vodka**
**soda**
**ice**
**To decorate: cucumber slice & mint**

*Put the cucumber, lime juice and vodka in a blender and whizz till almost a purée. Serve on the rocks topped up with soda and decorated with a slice of cucumber and a sprig of mint.*

## Hair of the Dog

This very English expression means that for those who have had too much the night before, a little more of the same will make them feel better. It rarely does. However, there is a special drink of that name which apparently does the trick!

**1 measure Scotch whisky**
**$1^{1}/_{2}$ measures cream**
**$^{1}/_{2}$ measure honey**

*Shake all the ingredients together with ice and strain into a cocktail glass.*

*Cucumber Whizz*

*Hair of the Dog*

*Prairie Oyster*

## Prairie Oyster

*This is the non-alcoholic version; but you could add a little brandy if you really feel the need.*

**Worcestershire sauce**
**vinegar**
**tomato ketchup or sauce**
**1 egg yolk**
**cayenne pepper**

*Mix together equal quantities of Worcestershire sauce, vinegar and ketchup. Add the unbroken yolk of the egg but do not stir. Sprinkle with cayenne pepper and down in one.*

## Yankee Doodle

**1 measure crème de banane**
**1 measure cognac**
**1 measure Royal Mint chocolate liqueur**

*Shake all three ingredients together over ice and strain into a cocktail glass.*

# Glossary

**Aperitif** – a drink before a meal designed to encourage the appetite: it could be either a commercial product or a mixed cocktail.

**Bitters** – spirits of varying strengths flavoured with roots and herbs, used in cocktails to add a kick or depth of flavour, or for medicinal purposes. Most common are Amer Picon, angostura, Campari, Fernet Branca, orange and peach bitters, Underberg.

**Cobbler** – originated in America as a drink for hot climates. Fill a highball glass with crushed ice, add 1 teaspoon fine sugar, one measure of gin, whisky or brandy, stir and decorate with seasonal fruit.

**Cooler** – a long mix of spirit, sugar or syrup and soda or ginger ale over crushed ice, decorated with fresh fruit.

**Cup** – a long refreshing drink made from wine, cider or fortified wine, topped up with mixers, with various added fruits or juices.

**Daisies** – these are variations on an original theme – spirit, raspberry syrup, lemon juice, crushed ice and fruit.

**Egg Nog (Noggin or Grog)** – variations on a mix of brandy, rum, milk, egg and sugar sprinkled with nutmeg. Other spirits can be used and they are usually iced.

**Fix** – a mix of spirit, lemon, sugar, water and fruit on crushed ice in a highball.

**Fizz** – five parts chilled sparkling wine to one part grenadine or other fruit syrup.

**Flip** – favourite sailor's drink which was originally made with rum, brandy or port with egg and sugar, shaken and then sprinkled with nutmeg or ginger.

**Frappé** – well iced drinks, usually liqueurs or spirits, served over finely crushed ice and drunk with a straw.

**Gomme Syrup** – a sugar syrup made by dissolving 2 cups of white sugar in 1 cup of water by simmering them together briefly. Used for adding extra sweetness to cocktails.

**Highball** – a spirit, liqueur or wine served in a long tumbler with ice and topped up with soda or ginger ale. The glass also takes its name from the drink. It is said to have originated in St. Louis in the late 19th century based on the fact that on many railroads, a ball hoisted up on a pole was a signal to an approaching train driver that he should speed up. Subsequently, it has come to mean a speedily made drink.

**Julep** – a long drink of spirit or liqueur, sugar and mint served in a frosted glass with crushed ice.

**Punch** – originated in India in the 18th century, based on rum and incorporating five different drinks. It has become a mix of many drinks, both non-alcoholic and alcoholic, carefully blended so that no one flavour predominates.

**Rickey** – a spirit served in a long glass over ice, topped up with soda and flavoured with lime or lemon to give a sharp, dry tang. A twist of rind should be added.

**Sangaree** – a combination of spirit, beer or wine mixed with lemon and sugar and served on the rocks (over ice cubes) with a grating of nutmeg.

**Shrub** – a slow maturing drink. Fruit such as currants or citrus fruits and sugar are boiled or left to marinade until ready to sieve through a jelly bag, then mixed with brandy or rum, bottled and left 6-8 weeks to mature.

**Sling** – a long drink of spirit, fruit juice or cordial topped up with soda.

**Smash** – a crush of mint leaves, a little water and cubed sugar is flavoured with rum, brandy, gin or whisky and served in an old-fashioned glass on the rocks with a slice of orange and twist of lemon rind.

**Sour** – spirit, lemon juice, sugar, angostura bitters and egg white, shaken.

**Straight up** – without ice.

**Toddy** – also known as Grog – a drink of spirit, lemon, sugar, cinnamon and either hot or cold water.

**Tom Collins** – lemon or lime juice, sugar, dry gin, shaken over ice, strained into a highball glass and topped up with soda.

# INDEX

*Page numbers in italics refer to illustrations*